Faith To Try Again

by
Richard Roberts

Albury Publishing
Tulsa, Oklahoma

Faith To Try Again
ISBN 1-88008-927-0
Copyright © by Richard Roberts
Tulsa, Oklahoma 74171

Published by Albury Publishing
P.O. Box 470406
Tulsa, Oklahoma 74147-0406

Introduction

Do you have a dream in your heart that has almost died because someone you love hurt you or something happened that devastated you? Have you allowed bitterness and discouragement to come into your heart? Maybe it's a dream you've had for just a few months, or a few years. Or maybe it's one you've had in your heart from your earliest memories. Maybe it's a dream like many of mine that I hardly dared to believe could ever happen to me—yet with all my heart I wanted to become reality.

I believe God places in our hearts His dream for our lives. If we will follow Him and trust Him to bring it to reality—regardless of how the circumstances in our lives look—regardless of who or what has hurt us—regardless of how many times we get knocked down and our dream seems to shatter to pieces right in front of our eyes—He will move heaven and earth on our behalf.

Maybe you feel like you'll fail before you ever begin because someone said to you as a child, "Well, he will never amount to anything," or "She will never do anything for God." My friend, I know how that feels.

But, praise God! The God I serve is the God who gives us faith to try again! He specializes in mending broken dreams, healing wounded hearts, and making something beautiful out of our lives.

No matter what has happened in your life in the past, you must know that it is never too late. You are never beyond hope. And there is nothing you could ever do to change the plan God prepared for you thousands of years before you were ever born—long before you ever made your first mistake.

Ephesians 2:10 says:

For we are his workmanship, created in Christ Jesus unto good works, which God hath before ordained that we should walk in them.

God has a purpose for your life! You are no mistake. You are not an accident just waiting to happen. You are His creation, not man's, so nothing you or anyone else thinks can change His plan.

If you feel like a failure, join the club! I have felt like a failure so many times it would take all my fingers and toes and maybe the hairs on my head to number them all. But that is not what matters. What does matter is that God loves you and has a plan and purpose for you.

If you have left a trail of failures behind you, God has this to say from Isaiah 43:18,19:

> *Remember ye not the former things, neither consider the things of old.*

FIRST THINGS FIRST

For what shall it profit a man,
if he shall gain the whole world,
and lose his own soul.
Mark 8:36

Behold, *I will do a new thing; now it shall spring forth; shall ye not know it? I will even make a way in the wilderness, and rivers in the desert.*

Isaiah 43:19

Failure in your past? Forget it! The Lord says, "Stop looking at your past. I have! Instead, let's look through the eyes of faith at your future. Let Me show you what I have planned. It is a good plan that will bring Me glory and you fulfillment."

I pray that as you read this book, you will see how the hopes and dreams you thought were long since buried in the ashes of your mistakes and failures can be resurrected in your heart to live again. You will realize when you turn your life over to our faith-restoring God, that He will take the broken pieces of your dream and give you back a plan for your life more wonderful than you ever dreamed possible! If He can do it for Richard Roberts, He can do it for you.

Now sit back for awhile and let's look at what God's Word has to say about your future. We serve a good God, and no matter what we have done, He is the God of another chance. He is the God who gives us Faith To Try Again!

> *For what shall it profit a man, if he shall gain the whole world, and lose his own soul?*

> *Mark 8:36*

All my life I've loved to sing. In fact, when I was just five years old, my dad stood me up on a chair in front of a crowded crusade in Baltimore, Maryland. It was there that I made my public singing debut with, "I Believe." As a teenager I continued to sing, but not in my dad's crusades. By then I had decided I didn't have time for God in my life. And I found I had less and less time for my family, too.

I became involved in all kinds of musical productions, plays, operas, and operettas at school and other places. I learned to play the guitar and began singing in pizza parlors around Tulsa. Then I moved into the nightclub circuit in town and across the state of Oklahoma.

During that time, a dream was birthed in my heart. It was not the dream God had given me of one day praying for the sick. It was a new dream of becoming a nightclub singer in Las Vegas. So I began to gear my life toward becoming a pro-fessional singer in the one place in this country that signals "success" in the eyes of the world.

There was no doubt in my mind that I had the talent to do it. Many people, including professional talent scouts, told me I did. As I walked in that direction, I soon became the lead singer in a very successful rock band.

I was on my way to success and I just didn't have time for anything else! I didn't realize it, but I was on a collision course.

During a vacation from school I went with my mother to dad's crusade in Roanoke, Virginia. And as it so happened, one of my dad's associates had been talking to him about my singing.

My dad had known about my love for singing, but he had never said much about it, at least not to me. We were in his hotel room one afternoon, and dad turned to me and said, "Richard, I've noticed how much singing you've been doing and I wondered if you would sing for me in the service tonight?"

It was a simple enough request, one that I would have been happy to oblige a few years earlier. But this time something came over me. I looked him straight in the eye and said, "No, dad, I don't want to."

"Why not?" he asked.

"I just don't want to," was my reply.

"Well, Richard, you have such a good voice, I'm sure everyone would like to hear you."

"Dad, I'm just not interested in singing tonight."

"Okay Richard, I understand. But do you have something against..."

"No, I'm just...just leave me alone," I said with finality in my voice.

That ended the discussion for that night, but the next night he asked me again.

"Richard, will you sing tonight?"

"No, dad, I don't want to."

And so it went the next night...and the next night...

He'd ask and I'd say no. He would ask again and I would say no. Gradually a wall began to build between the two of us. He'd push and I'd push back. He would push more and I would push back more. I didn't want him asking me to sing in his crusades. And I certainly didn't want him pressuring me about my relationship with Jesus Christ.

Actually, at that time I had no active relationship with Jesus. It had fallen by the wayside as I pursued my singing career. I knew I couldn't talk about a relationship that I didn't have, so the wall just got higher and higher. Then, finally, there was nothing left to say.

During my senior year in high school I applied to three different out-of-state universities. It was a great relief to me that I was accepted by all three, because Oral Roberts University had just opened the year before. And the last place in the world I wanted to go to school was Oral Roberts University! I mean, who wants to go to college where your dad's the founder and president?

All the way through high school, I had taken some pretty rough abuse because of dad's ministry. I'd had a lot of criticism about him and his healing ministry thrown at me and I was sick and tired of it.

So against my parents' wishes, I left Oklahoma and enrolled in an out-of-state university. I let it be known that I didn't want to be anywhere near the school my father was building. But the real reason I didn't want to go to ORU was because I didn't want God jammed down my throat.

It worked—for a while. No one talked to me about God or about singing for Jesus. I got to live in a coed dorm. I got to wear anything I wanted to wear and do anything I wanted to do. I went to bed when I wanted to and got up when I wanted to. If I didn't want to go to class, I didn't go. And no one cared what I had been drinking or putting into my system the night before.

I thought I was having the time of my life!

Then I went home to Tulsa for semester break. It was wintertime, cold, and dreary. But, as often happens in Oklahoma in mid-winter, one day the weather changed and it warmed up to spring-like temperatures. So dad and I decided to go out and play some golf together.

We went out to the golf course and were having a great time. It was just like the times I remembered from my childhood. But on the sixth green, as I was standing over a putt, he ruined everything. I'll never forget what happened.

"Richard, I'm having a seminar on campus tonight," dad said. "There will be hundreds of people there. Would you just come and sing one song?"

Suddenly that old fire began rising up on the inside of me. It was as if I had my fists doubled up and wanted to hit somebody. I looked at him with as much fire in my eyes as I could muster and snarled, "Look, dad, just get off my back. And don't ever mention God to me again!"

And that was one of the nicer things I said! But you know, my dad really surprised me that day. He said, "All right, Richard, I'll never mention God to you again unless you ask me to."

"Fine," I shot back. Then, suddenly the game had ended. So I left the golf course, got back into my car, and as fast as I could arrange it, left Tulsa and drove back to college for the second semester. "Well, that settles that once and for all," I thought, because I knew my dad was a man of his word. If he said he wouldn't mention God to me again unless I asked him, then he wouldn't.

I think that was probably the greatest favor my dad ever did for me, and I mean that in the right way. When he quit talking to me about God, I no longer had to listen to a man's voice, I began hearing another Voice instead. I didn't know who that Voice was at the time, but I knew I was hearing and feeling something different on the inside. It wasn't something I could describe to anyone else. Still, it was there.

I really believed that as soon as I got back to school everything would be fine. What I didn't know was that my special little world was about to fall apart right in front of my eyes.

Once back at school I immediately got sick and had to be hospitalized with a colon problem. Someone told me God caused my sickness. But I knew that was a lie because I knew sickness wasn't from God. Even though I didn't really have a relationship with God at that time, I had been raised in church and knew the Bible. I knew that God was a good God and that He never makes people sick. Sickness is an oppression of the devil.

How God anointed Jesus of Nazareth with the Holy Ghost and with power: who went about doing good, and healing all that were oppressed of the devil; for God was with him.

Acts 10:38

Even though I wasn't living out those beliefs, somewhere in my heart I still knew they were true. The Bible says,

Train up a child in the way he should go: and when he is old, he will not depart from it.

Proverbs 22:6

That's what my parents had done. So a strange thing happened to me when I was sick. For the first time in several years, I began to think about God!

It's amazing, isn't it. . . that when you get sick God seems to come across your mind? People sometimes go for years without thinking about Him until suddenly they get sick or find themselves in some other kind of jam. Then it all comes back to them.

That's what happened to me. Out of my sickness and pain came one of the greatest experiences of my life! This is when I discovered for the first time that our God is the God of a another chance. This discovery would begin to turn my life around.

Think about it.

Have you ever been on the wrong path in your life? Have you ever made a decision to go one way with your life when deep down in your heart you knew you were supposed to go another?

Maybe you've been caught in a relationship with someone like I was with my dad. You love them, but they just ask you too many questions about your relationship with the Lord. And you don't know how to answer them because, like me, you can't talk about a relationship you don't have.

My friend, when you choose to leave God out of your life—whether it's a willful decision like mine, or just because you never seem to have time to think about Him—you are making the greatest mistake of your life. Everything may appear to be going smoothly for a while. But the day will come when your back will be up against the wall just like mine was. The Bible says that sin is only pleasurable for a season and that in time it will tear you apart. (See Hebrews 11:25.) You would be surprised how important God can suddenly become to you when that finally happens.

The good news is that God will forgive you of your sin and turn your life around—if you will only repent and ask Him to.

IT'S NEVER TOO LATE

...and in the time of their trouble, when they cried unto thee, thou heardest them from heaven: and according to thy manifold mercies thou gavest them saviours, who saved them out of the hand of their enemies.
Nehemiah 9:27

FAITH TO TRY AGAIN

I *f we confess our sins, he is faithful and just to forgive us our sins, and to cleanse us from all unrighteousness.*

1 John 1:9

You ask, "Richard, is it really possible for me to get my life back on track and have a personal relationship with God, even though I've turned my back on Him all these years?"

I say, "Yes it is." He is the God who gives you Faith To Try Again!

...and in the time of their trouble, when they cried unto thee, thou heardest them from heaven: and according to thy manifold mercies thou gavest them saviours, who saved them out of the hand of their enemies.

Nehemiah 9:27

FAITH TO TRY AGAIN

While I was in the hospital I had a lot of time to think. I began thinking about all kinds of things. I thought I had friends at school, but when I got sick no one came to see me. And nobody prayed.

Suddenly I realized I was all alone. I felt like I was just a number, one of thousands of students. I found out what being really lonely feels like. So as I lay there in that bed, I began to call upon the God who I had run from. "If you'll heal me I'll give my life to you," I uttered in earnest prayer.

After my surgery was cancelled the next morning and I was released from the hospital—it began to dawn on me—I was healed! The Lord had healed me!

Then one day after I was back in my dormitory room resting between classes, I heard a Voice.

"You're in the wrong place," the Voice said.

I looked around and strangely enough, there was no one in the room with me! So I opened the closet door, looked under the bed, and still there was no one there.

I was determined to find out where that Voice was coming from, so I looked out the window to see if someone was hanging on the outside of the building. Then suddenly, the Voice spoke again.

"You're in the wrong place."

I just blurted out "If I'm in the wrong place, then where's the right place?"

"You're at the wrong university, you're supposed to be at Oral Roberts University," the Voice said this time.

I didn't know it then, but now I know it was the Holy Spirit speaking to my heart. I just knew I had heard a Voice saying something that I didn't want to hear! Some people may think that sounds crazy, but there was a Voice speaking inside of me somewhere and I heard it!

Ohhh...did I blow up at that! That was certainly the last thing I wanted to hear. Nevertheless, day after day and week after week I kept hearing that Voice say the same thing. It wouldn't leave me alone.

Sometimes people laugh when I tell this story because it sounds so strange. But I believe that's how the Holy Spirit deals with you. I not only believe it, I know it because that's how He dealt with me. He keeps speaking to your heart and speaking to your heart about what you should do. And He doesn't let go of you just because you say "no."

Finally one day I stopped fighting. I said, "All right, all right. I'll call ORU and see if they'll accept me." But before I called ORU I called my parents to ask their opinion. Their opinion? My, I was changing already! My mother said, "Richard, I don't know if they will accept you because of your habits. You can't smoke and drink and do other things like that and be an ORU student. Besides that," she said, "they may already be full for the next year."

"But, Mother," I said, "I can change. I can give up those habits."

After we finished talking I called the Oral Roberts University Director of Admissions. I said to him, "I know all the applications are probably in for next semester and you probably don't have room for me, but I'd like to come to ORU...."

But before I could even finish my sentence, he cut in, "Richard, we'll make a spot for you. You just come on." I guess they had more faith in me than I had in myself.

Well, now I'd really done it!

I finished the rest of the school year, then spent the summer working as a singer/actor at the Kansas City Starlight Theater. Then in September I moved back home and enrolled at ORU.

Believe me, it was one of the most difficult things I'd ever done! Talk about a culture shock! Overnight, I had to learn how to wear a shirt and tie to class. I even had to learn how to go to class and to the twice-weekly chapel services that are required. And I had to sign an Honor Code, pledging that I would keep all the rules and regulations of ORU.

"What a drag," I thought. But those were the rules, so I went along with them like everyone else. Before long I began to realize that the only thing that had changed about me was my physical proximity. I was still the same person with the same dream of being a nightclub singer in Las Vegas.

I hadn't been at ORU very long when both the Dean of Men and the Dean of Women had to call me in to discuss my "habits." I hadn't given up smoking or drinking. And there were many other things I'd gotten involved in at the other university that I was still doing, except at ORU it was a little more obvious. When you walk into your dorm room and you've been smoking, it's pretty easy for people to figure out who it is that smokes!

To make matters worse, one day I heard a rumor about me. I heard that from the moment I'd walked on the ORU campus, prayer groups had been praying for me.

Now that really made me angry!

It was one thing for me to do what that Voice had told me to do, but it was another thing altogether for these other people to get involved in it. They were praying for me to get saved! I thought, "The nerve of those other students. Why don't they just leave me alone!"

I'd walk down the hallway in my dorm and hear a group of guys praying in one of the rooms. Sometimes I'd hear my name being called out to God in prayer. I really didn't like it. I didn't want those people praying for me or getting involved in my life.

But one day something began to stir in me. When you have a group of people praying for you who really care for you and you know it, it gets to you.

People would come up to me on campus or in the dorm and put their arm around me. They'd give me a pat on the back and say they cared about me...and I knew they really did. I could feel their concern and I liked that.

Soon I found out something very important. I found out that my heart wasn't "cold as stone" like I thought it was. I wanted those people to care about me! No one at that other university had ever done those things. There, I was just a number...no one really knew me.

So the way everyone at ORU treated and cared about me began to ignite a new fire in my heart.

One Sunday afternoon I went home to talk to my parents about what was on my mind...about how miserable I had been feeling about my life. Dad was out of town conducting a crusade in Los Angeles, but my mother was there. So I began to pour my heart out to her like I hadn't done in many years. She put her arms around me as I talked, and when I finished she said, "Richard, you're never going to be happy and fulfilled until you have a personal relationship with Jesus Christ."

Suddenly I knew exactly what she meant! I'd never really had a personal relationship with Jesus since I was old enough to make a real commitment of my life to Him. And I knew I had to do it that day.

So at the age of nineteen, just two weeks before my twentieth birthday, I put my head in my mother's lap like I'd done so many times as a little boy, and I repeated a very simple sinner's prayer after her. When I finished confessing my sins and asking God to forgive me, I felt for the first time in my life that I could make it.

FAITH TO TRY AGAIN

In that one moment, my life was completely changed.

Think about it.

Would you like to meet this God who gave me faith to try again? Would you like to have the power in your life to change those things you know aren't right? Deuteronomy 4:29 says:

But if from there you seek the Lord your God, you will find him if you look for him with all your heart and with all your soul (NIV).

And in 2 Corinthians 5:17 it says,

Therefore if any man be in Christ, he is a new creature: old things are passed away; behold, all things are become new.

You can have a brand-new life today when you accept Jesus into your heart. You can have your faith renewed to make your life what you've always wanted it to be. Let me lead you in a simple prayer of confession. Will you pray this prayer out loud?. . .

Oh, Lord, be merciful to me, a sinner. I ask Your forgiveness for all the wrong things I've done in my life and I ask You to cleanse me of my sin. Lord I repent and turn my back on Satan's plan for my life. I believe You sent Your Son Jesus to die on the cross for my sin and then raised Him from the dead so I could have a brand new life. I accept Him now as my personal Lord and Savior. Jesus, I invite You to come into my life today and to make my life what You would have it to be. Thank You, Lord, for dying for me, for loving me, and for giving me faith to try again. In Jesus' name, I am going to make it! Amen.

I thank God you have prayed this prayer! The greatest miracle of all is the salvation of a soul...because only God knows what He can do with a life that is truly "sold out" to Him.

FAITH TO FORGIVE
YOURSELF

*...forgive others, even as you
yourself have been forgiven.
Luke 6:37*

As we have therefore opportunity, let us do good unto all men...

Galatians 6:10

Let's get one thing straight. Once you are born again there are no promises that life will be a bowl of cherries. In fact, after receiving Jesus as my Lord, I turned in one set of problems for another. We all have made mistakes in our past and sometimes find it hard to forgive ourselves for things done out of ignorance. A painful divorce while I was very young is one of those things I had to move past in my life.

Thank God that was not the end of my story. Through many years of suffering and heartache, I came to know the love and grace of God in a way I might never have known otherwise. Time passed and with God's help and grace, I did get on with my life and the call He gave me.

FAITH TO TRY AGAIN

It wasn't easy, believe me. At the age of thirty I was still a young man with the normal desires that any young man has. So after awhile I began to pray that the Lord would send a woman into my life so that I might have a marriage of love, honor, and respect. I prayed that God would send me someone I could support who would support me and the work that God had called me to do.

By this time the Lord was also dealing with me about a preaching ministry in addition to my singing. Therefore, during the time I was single I answered God's call to preach with a resounding YES. When I did, a great anointing came upon me to preach and teach God's Word. And I had a deep desire for a wife who would understand and support me in the full call that God had on my life.

While all this was going on in my life, God began dealing with a young woman far away in Florida. Her name was Lindsay Salem.

Lindsay's family had lived in Michigan when she was a little girl. They had been Partners with my dad's ministry for years. Before her father died when Lindsay was only twelve, Mr. Salem had been friends with my dad's close associate in the ministry, Lee Braxton. And before Mr. Salem died, Lee had arranged for my dad to phone Mr. Salem to pray for him while he was in the hospital.

Lindsay's family was very close-knit, and of course, her father's death was very difficult for her to handle. During that time in her life, she began watching my dad regularly on TV. She began writing letters to him and became a Partner with him in his ministry. In fact, she has always said that if it had not been for my dad's teaching, she might not have made it through that difficult time as a teenager without her father. Of course, I didn't know any of these things until we met many years later.

After her father's death, Lindsay's family moved to Florida. She went to high school and college there and graduated from Rollins College in 1978 with very good grades and a desire to go to law school. From the time she was just a little girl, Lindsay had dreamed of becoming a lawyer, but she wanted to go to a law school where the teaching wouldn't conflict with her faith in Jesus Christ. She knew that ORU's law school would open in 1979, one year later, so she decided to wait.

While she waited, Lindsay worked in a law office to get as much practical experience as she could. Then in August of 1979, she was accepted to ORU's law school and relocated from Winter Park, Florida, to Tulsa to be part of the first O.W. Coburn School of Law class.

On the way to Tulsa, the Lord began speaking to her about a young man named Richard Roberts. Now you've got to remember that

Lindsay had always wanted to become a lawyer. She had absolutely no desire to get married at that time in her life. And she was completely taken by surprise when the Lord kept bringing my name and face before her during her long drive to Tulsa.

She couldn't figure out why thoughts about me kept coming to her. As a teenager watching my dad's program on TV, she had viewed me as an older, married man. (Actually, I'm only seven years older than Lindsay.) She had only seen me on TV a few times since she learned I was divorced. And each time she did she seemed to sense a deep loneliness about me and that I'd been through something very painful. All she could make out of it was that perhaps the Lord wanted her to help me get over whatever I'd been through that had been so painful.

Lindsay had not been on campus more than a few days before she met a law-school classmate who just "happened" to be a good friend of mine.

By this time, Lindsay was beginning to feel a very strong attraction to me. The Lord had continued to bring my face and name to her mind every day. Then one night during the first week of school, my friend arranged for Lindsay to meet me after a service in which I preached to the ORU students, faculty, and staff.

I preached on the story of David and Goliath. During my sermon, I asked those in the audience to think of the three biggest giants they were currently facing in their lives. Then I prayed for those needs to be met.

After the service, I went backstage to meet this girl from Florida my friend had been telling me about. He introduced us, and immediately I noticed how attractive she was. Lindsay said she had really enjoyed my message, so I said to her, "What did you enjoy about it?"

"I liked the part about your biggest giant," she replied.

Then when I asked her, "What's your biggest giant?" she looked me straight in the eyes and said, "You are."

I literally took a step backward as what she had said sunk in. I smiled and tried to be polite. Then I looked over at my friend as if to say, "Thanks a lot for introducing me to this nut!"

We stood there for a couple of minutes before I excused myself and walked away with my friend. As we walked out the door I said, "Why did you introduce me to her? What have I ever done to her? I've never seen her before tonight!" We both just kind of laughed and went on, and I thought that was the end of that!

But as the days began to pass, I found that I couldn't stand the suspense any longer. I had to know just what that girl meant by saying I was her biggest giant. Lindsay was living in our graduate housing community so I picked up the phone and called her to find out what I'd done to cause that response.

When she answered I said, "Will you please explain to me your remark the other night about my being your biggest giant?"

So she rather reluctantly began to tell me the story of how for some time the Lord had been bringing my name and my face to her mind. She told me how she had been praying for me. She told me that in the last few months as she watched me on TV she had seen the loneliness in my face. And that the Lord must have placed a special burden on her heart for me.

I still didn't understand what she was talking about. So I said, "Well then, what do you mean I'm your biggest problem?"

Then she said, "Richard, you don't understand at all. I've dreamed of being a lawyer all my life. I want to go to law school and practice law. That's why I came here! But the Lord keeps dealing with me about having some kind of relationship with you. And if that happens, it's going to throw all of my plans clear off."

Thinking of how unusual our relationship had already been, I said to her, "Well, I'm not so sure I want a relationship with you."

In the end, we both decided we'd like to meet again, so I asked her out and we had our first date on August 27, 1979.

Today, Lindsay and I have been married for more than fifteen years. She still tells me and other people that she fell in love with me the very first night we went out, which was hard for her to reconcile. She even asked the Lord, "How could You let me fall in love with Richard Roberts when You know I've had a dream all my life of being a lawyer?" She knew enough about my life and work for the Lord to know that if she married me, the law career she had always dreamed of would not be compatible with being my wife.

But more than anything else, Lindsay loved the Lord and wanted His will for her life. She knew that whatever plan He had for her life would be where she would find the most fulfillment. Needless to say she never would have married me without knowing it was God's will.

On the other hand, I was also hesitating, but for very different reasons. Having been through a divorce the year before, I was really seeking the Lord about this new relationship. I knew that if I were to remarry, all hell would probably break loose from all sides. Critics would come out of the woodwork who, until then, had not spoken up about my divorce. I also knew that in any future marriage I needed to have a Bible wife in every sense of the word. I needed a woman who would stand beside me in the ministry and help me fulfill God's calling on my life. I had to know that our relationship was what God had for my life, not just what Richard Roberts thought he wanted.

Lindsay and I shared these feelings with each other and prayed about it many times during the months we dated. We were absolutely certain that any future happiness we might have together would depend upon our first knowing that God had brought us together, and that it was His intention for us to be man and wife.

I want to share with you how God confirmed over and over to us that our relationship had been ordained of Him.

The first thing that happened involved Lindsay's family. When I took her back to her apartment after our first date, she called her mother. She's very close to her family, as I am to mine, and she wanted to tell them what had happened.

Up until this time she had not told her mom anything about meeting me. But when her mother answered the phone and Lindsay said, "Mom, guess where I went tonight?" her mother very calmly replied, "You went out with Richard Roberts."

Well, needless to say, Lindsay was shocked.

"How in the world did you know that?" she asked.

"Well, I pray to the same Lord you do, Lindsay. And He told me that's what you'd be doing tonight."

What a surprise! But it really helped Lindsay to know that God had already spoken to her mother about us. She has a great deal of confidence in her mom's judgment, and I think their conversation about our date eased her mind that this was indeed of God.

Lindsay and I began dating regularly, and our relationship began to flourish. During my divorce and the months after, I had suffered from an ulcer. I had been on medication, still it would continually flare up. I prayed about it and others prayed for me, but I couldn't seem to get completely healed. Sometimes the medicine would work and sometimes it wouldn't. But within the first two weeks of our dating, the ulcer completely disappeared.

After about three months of dating, I knew that I was beginning to fall in love with Lindsay. That concerned me, not because of her, but because of me. I was worried about the hard road of criticism that would face us if we were to marry. So I began to pray about it.

By this time I was 31 years old. I wanted to remarry and have a family. In my heart of hearts I knew God was not a God of punishment, but of mercy. Just because I had made a mistake when I was very young, He would not punish me for the rest of my life. I didn't believe He wanted me to live as a single man always subject to temptation.

So I began to ask God what He wanted me to do. This was very serious to me, and I needed an answer.

"God, do You want me to live alone for the rest of my life and live a life of celibacy?" I asked. I was willing to do that if I really knew that was what He wanted me to do.

But I also prayed, "God, I don't believe You want me to be lonely and miserable. I believe You are the God of another chance. You were the God of another chance when Peter denied You three times. And I believe if Judas would have only run to the cross and thrown his arms around Your feet crying, 'Jesus, I'm sorry for selling You out. I know I made a mistake, please forgive me,' that You would have been the God of another chance for Judas as well."

Then I thought again about the Samaritan woman at the well who had had five husbands...who after coming to the Lord Jesus, was sent by Him to her town to be an evangelist. He didn't condemn her to a life of punishment for her past. So why would He do so to me?

As I meditated on these things, the most wonderful feeling came over me. I came to the conclusion that even if people were against me, God was for me! God didn't want me to be unhappy or alone for the rest of my life. He knew the anointing on me to preach was growing, and that I needed a wife who would be a helpmate.

It was a wonderful realization! So Lindsay and I began talking about marriage. I asked her if she was prepared for the onslaught of criticism that she would receive as my wife from people who might misunderstand my remarriage. I also brought up the possibility of it coming from people who were close to us.

Lindsay said she knew she would have the support of her family and that this would be a tremendous help to her coping with the criticism.

As we planned and talked about the future, something really incredible happened to us that was impossible to ignore.

Lindsay and I had always attended the twice-weekly chapel service at ORU during the time we were dating—but never together. She would sit with the graduate students and I would sit on the platform with those in the university administration. At this point only a few people knew we were dating, and none of them knew how serious our relationship had become.

One day in that fall of 1979 our chapel speaker was Kenneth Hagin. He certainly was not one of the people who knew!

After he preached in our chapel service he began to prophesy. Now I had known Brother Hagin for many years. He was a man I deeply loved and admired and in whose ministry I believed. I had seen him prophesy many times in my life and knew that when he was operating in the office of the prophet he was always "right on."

But this time as he prophesied, he turned to me. Though he didn't speak in specifics, I knew exactly what he was talking about. He said to me, "That thing which you have been praying about doing, and you've been concerned about what people are going to think and say and do, it is of God. Do it and don't worry about what they think or say or do."

Well, I looked out in the crowd where Lindsay was sitting and she looked like she was going to slide underneath her seat! We were probably the only two people in the building who knew what Brother Hagin was talking about. She knew exactly what he meant...and she knew that I knew. It was then that, without a shadow of doubt, we both knew it was right in the sight of the Lord for us to be married.

After we were married, I had the chance to talk to him about it one day. I said, "Brother Hagin, I know when the Spirit of prophecy comes upon you or other men and women of God that later you are often not aware of all that you said. That day in chapel when you gave the word of prophecy to me, did you know the ramifications of what the Lord was having you say?"

A big grin came across his face as Brother Hagin said, "Well, Richard, I'll tell you this, I could have even told you her name. But I didn't think it was appropriate right then."

What a wonderful confirmation from the Lord Brother Hagin's word of prophecy had been to us! He didn't know Lindsay; he'd never even met her. But God used him to tell us that our marriage plans were not just good plans—they were His plans.

So with the peace of God in our hearts, we set the date for our wedding. Lindsay was committed to our marriage. She returned home to Florida where we planned to be wed, but Lindsay was never sure whether Richard Roberts would really show up!

She knew I was deeply concerned about the criticism we would encounter after we married. And she knew there might still be the possibility that I would back out of our plans at the last minute. Today she will tell you she was never so relieved in her life as that night when the plane landed in Orlando and she saw my pair of cowboy boots coming down the stairs!

What she didn't know was there had been a chance that I might not have come. After she returned home I spent some time with the leadership of the Oral Roberts Ministry, talking to them about my desire to remarry. It was one of the hardest things I've ever done. But I wanted them to know I cared about how they felt about our plans. I went to them individually and asked them to pray with me.

Then I gathered the leaders of the university, the City of Faith, and the evangelistic association together in a private meeting. This took place several days before I was to fly to Florida. I asked them to keep everything confidential and publicly said, "I realize that you don't really have the right to say 'no' to my remarriage. But as my co-laborers in the ministry, I'm giving you that right. I'm asking for your blessing on our marriage...and I will abide by your decision."

And I meant it. I felt this could be one last confirmation of support that Lindsay and I needed before we married.

To my joy, they came and threw their arms around me. They applauded me for keeping my life right before the Lord during the year that I had been single. In essence, they said, "We've seen you and Lindsay together and we have a good feeling about this marriage. We support you 100 percent. "OF COURSE YOU HAVE OUR BLESSING!"

Finally, in my eyes, there were no more hurdles to overcome and I knew that we should be married as soon as possible. My family felt good about it, Lindsay's family felt good about it, and the top people in our ministry felt good about it. So without announcing it to anyone, we were married in the chapel of the Rollins College campus on January 11, 1980.

God had not only given me another chance at living, He had given me faith to love again.

I'm not going to mislead anybody on this point. When you decide to follow God and shut a deaf ear to the threat of the enemy, it by no means keeps him from attacking you on all sides when you step out to obey.

What I will tell you, is if you keep your eyes on Jesus and keep walking forward, day after day, you will find yourself moving closer to each new destination He sets before you.

When Lindsay and I were married, we knew it would be tough. Anyone in the public eye knows they have very little privacy as they go about the job of living. But to those in full time ministry, especially those of us who proclaim the Gospel of a healing, loving, providing

God, we are not just under the media's staring eyes. They take great pleasure in cutting us up, pasting us down, and looking at us under their out-of-focus microscope!

They tried to find anything they could. "Oral Roberts Son Marries Woman 10 Years His Junior." They had photographers at what we thought was our private wedding.

But none of that mattered to us. We went to Israel for our honeymoon, and Lindsay has been right beside me in the ministry ever since.

Think about it.

In whatever failure you're facing, have you accepted your part of the blame yet? Have you admitted to yourself and to God that you made a mistake? Maybe you have a long history of making bad decisions and you think that God can never forgive you and give you another chance. I believe with all my heart and I speak with the confidence of knowing what the Word of God says, that there is nothing you could have done or ever will do that God cannot and will not forgive. You simply have to ask Him.

You see, God can never forgive you if you don't get down on your knees and ask Him to. That's something He cannot do for you. God has already done His part in making forgiveness available to you when He sent Jesus to the cross. Now you have to do your part and reach out to receive that forgiveness. You may want to pour out your heart to Him concerning your years of mistakes. Or it may be as simple as just saying one or two words that you mean from the bottom of your heart, such as..."Jesus...O.K.!"

FAITH TO TRY AGAIN

That's what a guest on my daily TV program said to the Lord when he knew he could no longer make it in life without Him. After years and years of pain, he came to the end of himself...just as you may be at the end of yourself right now. With tears streaming down his cheeks, he lifted his hands up to heaven and shouted, "Jesus...O.K.!"

With those two simple words, the young man's life was miraculously transformed. He is now preaching the gospel, praying for the sick, and winning thousands of souls to the Lord.

Now that doesn't mean God is going to call you into a healing ministry when you turn your past failures over to Him. But it does mean He has something more for you to do...something that's just right for you. And someone special to love and to love you, the way I love Lindsay and she loves me.

God's not through blessing you, my friend. God's not through giving you the desires of your heart—or helping you fulfill the dreams you've had all your life.

FAITH TO SUCCEED

*...forgetting those things which
are behind, and reaching forth
unto those things which are before.
I press toward the mark for the prize
of the high calling of God in Christ Jesus.*
Philippians 3:13

Everything is possible for him who believes.

Mark 9:23 NIV

As I look back now, I see that it was only after my greatest failures that my life really began. And like you, I never would have believed it possible for God to turn things around.

But it happened...and it's possible for you my friend. It can happen right now...if you'll take that first step by getting down on your knees before God. Ask Him to forgive you. Then believe that He has. You can trust God. He's the God of another chance!

I press toward the mark for the prize of the high calling of God in Christ Jesus.

Philippians 3:13

The first thing I did—and the first thing you must do, my friend— was to get down on my knees before God. I admitted what I'd done wrong and where I'd failed. I asked God to forgive me. And I determined not to make the same mistakes again. I told Him I didn't believe He wanted to throw me away because of my mistakes, and that He still had something He wanted to do with my life. Then God began to turn my life around.

He brought my beautiful wife Lindsay into my life, who stands beside me in my work for the Lord. Lindsay loves me with a love only God could have given her. Then He called me to begin preaching His Word and praying for the sick. I had never done this before. For many years I had sung for the Lord in my dad's ministry, but I'd never felt called to preach. I had always loved to see people healed in my dad's crusades. And I had dreamed a child's dream of perhaps one day praying for the sick in my own ministry. I had just never allowed myself to believe that it was really possible.

But God knew it was! He had put that desire in my heart! It was part of His "good plan" for my life.

You see, God saw me as a healing evangelist long before I could ever see it myself. He saw me as what He had created me to be rather than what I had become in my own eyes. I saw myself as a failure, but God saw me as a success!

And God sees you as the success He created you to be, even if you see yourself as a failure!

If you've failed, my friend, don't try to hide from it. Don't try to deny it. Don't try to run from it, or you may be hiding, denying, and running the rest of your life. Turn your failure over to God. Confess your mistakes to Him and ask for His forgiveness.

Then believe that God has forgiven you. Quit worrying about what other people think about you and listening to the devil say you're just no good and never will be. That's a lie!

FAITH TO TRY AGAIN

Link up with God's plan for your life. Walk in the "good works" that He has destined you to walk in. I promise you, based on the Word of God and on my own personal experience, you will begin to see yourself as the wonderful success God sees you as, and has always intended you to be.

Make the following confession over and over until you begin to believe it—then say it some more untill you are fully convinced:

"I can know God sees me as a success even when I see myself as a failure."

Set your heart and mind that with God's help you will get out of the failure you're currently in and get into doing what God has always planned for you. His plans always bring success!

Think about it.

Have you ever noticed how people are always parking their cars where they don't belong? We park in front of driveways and too close to fire hydrants. Sometimes when there isn't room anywhere else, we even double-park right in the middle of the street! In fact, we are so inclined to park where we don't belong, "no parking" signs line our streets. *Admit your failures, but don't live in them.*

In addition to parking our cars where they don't belong, we sometimes park our lives where they don't belong. Quite honestly, the greatest parking problem we have as human beings is parking beside our failures.

Jesus understands how devastating failure can be. He doesn't want us to sit in the middle of our defeats and failures, letting something that happened in the past prevent us from achieving success today. I like to think of God's Word of forgiveness and restoration to me as a sign He's posted by my failures that reads:

> no
> parking

You know, there have been times when I felt like crawling into a hole and dying. There have been times when I wanted to throw up my hands and quit...when I felt like my life was over.

But in the midst of those times, I felt something else burning within me that let me know God wasn't finished with me yet. So I resisted the temptation to let those feelings of failure affect the rest of my life. And I made up my mind that I wouldn't park beside my failures. I knew I couldn't redeem the past, but that God could. I made up my mind not to park beside it.

Now remember, not parking beside your failures doesn't mean you don't admit your mistakes and failures. You just refuse to let them be a hindrance. By repenting and receiving forgiveness, you open your mind and heart to God, and He can teach you from them.

When you are truly sorry and ask God to give you another chance, He always does. God doesn't hang on to the sins you've confessed to hit you over the head with every time you do something wrong from then on. When God forgives, He forgets. In Hebrews 8:12 He tells us:

...their sins and their iniquities will I remember no more.

God wants us to learn from our mistakes and our failures, but He doesn't want us to live in the shadow of them. He doesn't want us to "park" beside them because He knows that will paralyze us. It will keep us from all He wants us to do.

When that dawns on the inside of you, as it did me, I believe you will do as I did. You will pick yourself up, dust yourself off and say, "God, whatever You have for my life, I will do it." You will put your life on "go" again. You will discover that some of God's greatest blessings come after our greatest failures and defeats...if we will only give those failures and defeats to Him.

I had been through many circumstances, mostly caused by my rebellion to God and my call to the ministry. But God didn't throw me out with the trash. He established a deeper relationship with me and a fresh love for His Word. Out of that new intimacy He gave me Lindsay and called me to preach and to pray for the sick. If I'd given up and laid down in my failure, I never would have known the tremendous blessings God still had in store for my life, and through my life—to the lives of many others.

Don't be afraid to try again!

You may be in the midst of a failure right now; a failure you would like to sweep under the carpet; a failure that is keeping you from going on with what God has planned for your life. If so, Jesus is speaking to you today. He is saying, "Don't park beside your failures. Don't give up. Put your faith in Me and try again."

You know, it takes courage to try again. The devil would like to use your failures to paralyze you with fear. He tries to tell you that if you try again, you'll only fail again. But you don't have to make the same mistakes twice. Jesus tells you that:

> *"As far as the east is from the west, so far hath he [God] removed our transgressions from us."*

Psalm 103:12

He can wipe the slate clean. He can change your heart.

Listen to these words from a song I often sing on my daily TV program. Take them to heart as God's word to you today:

People may judge you and you may even judge yourself, but this I know, God is for you...and He's saying to you...

Try again.

Try again.

Things won't turn out like before.

Just try again.

THE AWESOME POWER
OF FORGIVENESS

Do not repay evil with evil or insult with insult, but with blessing, because to this you were called so that you may inherit a blessing.
1 Peter 3:9 NIV

And be ye kind one to another, tenderhearted, forgiving one another even as God for Christ's sake hath forgiven you.

Ephesians 4:32

I believe what I'm about to say next is going to hit you like a freight train! It's going to strike deep in your heart because this message gets right down to where we all live. I've seen people, and I know you've seen them too, who always seem to be catching it from every angle. They are always beset by some kind of struggle or satanic attack, but somehow they keep landing on their feet. How do they do it? They are praying people! No matter how the devil lashes out at them, they keep their eyes fixed on the Lord!

I can identify with that, because I know what it's like to be hit, to be struck with words until you feel like giving up.

FAITH TO TRY AGAIN

I know what it feels like to be lied about, to have the facts twisted, and to be misrepresented by the media in their scurrilous reports. Ours is a ministry that has been lambasted, mocked, and ridiculed many times over the years. Our funeral will never have to be preached because it's been preached over and over for the last 45 years! But we are still alive and standing strong for the Good News of Jesus! The devil has shot his arrows and flung his stones, but I say, "Let the devil take his best shot, and we will still be standing for the healing power of Jesus Christ!"

And when ye stand praying, forgive,...

Mark 11:25

Now let's get down to where the rubber meets the road. You and I both know there are times in your life when you're struck in a terrible way by something that cuts you to the very core! I mean, it feels like you've been stabbed with a knife, and if you're not careful, that hurt will grab hold of you and you will find yourself harboring bitter feelings against someone.

Unforgiveness is an awful thing! It starts small, but when you hold it inside, it begins to fester and the next thing you know, you're not in a mood to forgive! Little by little, it permeates your entire being. It possesses your thoughts day and night until bitterness takes root in your soul and begins to gnaw at you. Then that root of bitterness releases its deadly poisons not only in your life, but in the lives of everyone around you! The Bible says,

> *Looking diligently...lest any root of bitterness springing up trouble you, and thereby many be defiled;*
>
> Hebrews 12:15

FAITH TO TRY AGAIN

How well I remember when Lindsay and I lost our precious newborn son, Richard Oral. Not long after, someone wrote us and said, "The reason your son died is because you got a divorce and married Lindsay. You deserved to have your baby die!" I can't begin to describe how words like that can cut your heart out! But what did Jesus say?

And when ye stand praying, FORGIVE, if ye have ought against any: that your Father also which is in heaven may forgive you your trespasses.

Mark 11:25

Lindsay and I didn't have a choice! The words of Jesus compelled us to pray and to forgive that person!

How many times must you and I forgive? I'm reminded of how the apostle Peter addressed that very same question to the Lord one day,

"How many times must I forgive—seven times?" (See Matthew 18:21.) The mere fact that Peter asked this particular question and attached the number seven to it indicates to me that he probably had forgiven someone seven times already—and now he was fed up with it!

In my own imagination, I can see Jesus looking with pity at the impetuous, hot-tempered apostle as He replied, "Peter, you must forgive seventy times seven!" Or in other words, "you must live in a continual state of forgiveness!"

God turned the captivity of Job when he forgave his friends!

My heart is drawn to the very moving story of Job, because he was a man who had countless reasons not to forgive! Everywhere he turned, Job suffered devastating losses. He actually experienced the horror of seeing all he held precious and dear being destroyed.

There was a time when Job slept on soft pillows beneath hanging chandeliers—he had it all. But like a bolt of lightning, the devil swept through his life with relentless fury! Thieves plundered Job's cattle and oxen. His donkeys and mules were stolen. And his servants were brutally murdered!

In one terrible day, Job's worst fear was realized as the lives of all of his children were tragically snuffed out. Even his wife began to plead with him to curse God and die! But it was his friends who would deal him a final, almost-crushing blow. They accused him before God, and declared that his horrible, wretched condition had come upon him because of some secret sin in his life!

Now Job could have turned his back on the Lord. He could have shaken his fist at the Almighty for allowing Satan to cut this wide swath of destruction through his life! He could have let bitterness toward his friends eat away at his very soul. But the Bible says:

And the Lord turned the captivity of Job, when he prayed for his friends: also the Lord gave Job twice as much as he had before.

Job 42:10

The instant Job forgave his friends for their cruel words, God reached down and lifted him up out of that horrible pit. God put him in the middle of His mighty stream of blessing and blessed Job DOUBLE in his latter years of life!

Forgiveness is the Bible way!

Think About It.

My friend, I'm dealing with reality today because I want to help you get down to the root of your deliverance! And I ask you...have you forgiven others, or are you carrying unforgiveness in your heart? Or maybe you haven't been able to forgive yourself for some tragic mistake from the past that's been haunting you. Remember, our God is a merciful, forgiving God. So why don't you ask Him to forgive you and let Him cast that sin into the deepest fathom of the sea! (See Micah 7:19.)

Or maybe you are harboring bitterness against the Lord Himself because you've been struck by a dreadful loss. Maybe someone or something has been snatched out of your life. If so, you've got to let it go. You've got to deal with that root of bitterness or it will literally drain the life out of you.

Have you been lied about, lied to, criticized, or ostracized? Have you been abused or brutalized? Have you been kicked out, cussed out or left out? If so, instead of panicking or running in terror, begin to pray! Instead of beating your fists in the air or striking back at those who have hurt you, lift your heart and lift your voice in prayer to Almighty God!

When you bow your head before the Lord in prayer and begin to cry out to Him, you can expect the spiritual power of Jesus Christ to come upon you. You will feel His presence flowing through your soul! Because as you pray, the love of God is shed abroad in your heart as the Bible teaches in Romans 5:5. And when you arise from that place of prayer, you will find you are able to forgive those who have said those terrible things against you. You will be able to bless those who have persecuted you, and pray for those who have committed all manner of evil against you. You will be able to lay those people at the feet of Jesus! Now that's the Bible way!

TURNING IT AROUND

And we know that all things work together for good to them that love God, to them who are the called according to his purpose.
Romans 8:28

For whom He did foreknow, He also did predestinate to be conformed to the image of His Son...

Romans 8:29

In 1983 the Lord spoke to me one day as I was praying. He gave me the names of forty nations and regions of the world that I was to visit. I have now been to many of these places and held large crusades, some before the head political leaders of the countries. There are many testimonies of changed lives through countless miracles Jesus did while we were there.

This is a testimony to God of not only His faithfulness to fulfill His promises to us, but of His sense of humor if you really think about it. When I was a young man trying to find my way through life, I wanted to be a singer in night clubs far away from the responsibilities of a godly life. I wanted nothing to do with God or His university that my father helped to establish. I certainly never wanted to go traveling around the world to many of the desolate, poverty stricken, and war torn countries I am now visiting. I wanted what I thought was freedom.

But God had another plan. God had another purpose. God had a vision so much greater than I could have ever imagined—ever hoped for. He waited patiently while I ran around trying my level best to accomplish my dreams. Finally, because of the wear and tear of stress that my plan took on my body and mind, I ended up in the hospital. I was at the end of my rope emotionally with no where to turn but God.

And you know what? God picked me up like the prodigal son! God said He was so glad I had come to Him, brushed me off, put new clothes on my back and put hope in my heart. In that restoration process, God gave me a revelation of His grace that has carried me to this day. It has helped tens of thousands of people through the television shows around the world and in my personal visits to so many hurting places throughout the globe.

I went from a kid who was running away form ORU and God—to a man who not only received two degrees from there, but is now the President and CEO! I wanted to sing in the glitzy night clubs of Las Vegas and make a name for myself with a pile of worldly riches. And now I travel the globe and minister with my wife Lindsay on daily television. Together we glorify Jesus' name and spread the riches of His gospel message with healing power to hurting people around the world. What a turn around! What a God! What a sense of humor!

FAITH TO TRY AGAIN

Think about it.

Are you at a point of giving up or giving in? Maybe you know God has forgiven you for your mistakes, even rebellion in your past. But you have this idea that you blew God's original plan for your life and now there's just no way you could get back on track for His plan for your life. I have three words for you: BELIEVE GOD AGAIN!

God is in the redeeming business.

Who gave Himself on our behalf that He might redeem us...from all iniquity and purify for Himself a people...eager and enthusiastic about [living a life that is good and filled with] beneficial deeds.

Titus 2:14 AMP

God loves the hard core cases. When He turns around hopeless situations, it is a knock out punch to the devil that sends his demons and plans for his kingdom reeling in defeat.

So don't give up—look up. Don't give in, dig in—to God's Word. See how its stories of people whose lives were filled with bumbling and stumbling were turned around when they turned it all over to the Lord and began to trust in Him.

GOD WILL USE YOU

Looking unto Jesus the author and finisher
of our faith; who for the joy that was
set before him endured the cross.
Hebrews 12:2

...who for the joy that was set before him endured the cross...

One thing we need to keep in mind as we walk out our lives from day to day, is that God not only delights in getting blessing to us, He also delights in funneling His blessings through us.

Back in 1984, I received a letter from a man named Jerry Wood. Jerry had been in and out of prison on drug related problems over a period of 20 years. He was a heroin addict. One Sunday morning Jerry got out of bed needing his daily fix very bad. After he got dressed he went in the living room to finish getting ready and sat down in front of the TV that he had turned on earlier. It was tuned into our Sunday morning program, "Expect a Miracle: with Oral and Richard Roberts." We were on the show and I was led by the Spirit for someone who was a drug addict to be delivered from drugs. When Jerry put his hand on the TV set, God miraculously delivered him from the desire for drugs. His life was totally changed! He got a new job as the manager of the apartment complex where he lived—complete with a new apartment!

When Jerry wrote me about the way God had moved in his life, I read his letter and began to think of how wonderful it was that we had the Sunday morning program. If Jerry had been on his way out for drugs on Monday, or Tuesday or Wednesday or any other day the program wouldn't have been there. So God began dealing with Lindsay and me about a daily program to share the message that He wants to turn it around for millions of hurting people just like Jerry.

Think about it.

What if I would have given up at any point in my past because I thought it was just too hard to go on and face those who said I had stepped over the line and that God could no longer use me? Jerry and thousands of others like him might still be in desperate situations that they long to be freed from.

The same is true for you. God has a plan and purpose for your life too. Focusing on the people that God wants to help through you will keep you going. Jesus endured the cross for the joy that was set before Him. I believe that joy was for you and me. He endured the pain, suffering, and insults of those who mocked Him. But He didn't look at the men in front of Him who hated Him, He looked far into the future. He could see the good works He had called you and I to. He knew when He endured the cross that He was making available to us all the power we would need to do what He has destined us to do. There is power in the name of Jesus, and we do have the right to use His name.

So never give up. Never give in to the accusations of the enemy. A winner is not someone who never fails, he is someone who refuses to get back up when he falls. Take the strength the Lord offers you and get back in the race!

STRENGTH TO ENDURE

Strengthened with all might, according to his glorious power, unto all patience and longsuffering with joyfulness.
Colossians 1:11 NIV

...according to his glorious power, unto all patience and longsuffering with joyfulness...

Colossians 1:11

Many years after Lindsay and I started our daily television show, the Lord led us to go off for a time. We only had a vague idea of why God was leading. As I relate what happened to us over the next twenty-four months, you will see why we are glad we didn't know the reason for God's leading. I might have grabbed a suitcase, my wife and kids, and headed for some remote island to keep my sanity!

Now as I look back I can see the reason for the circumstances that He brought us through. But more importantly, I can see the transformation that has taken place on the inside of me that has spread to everyone around me. God has performed many miracles for my family, the university, and the ministry, but the greatest of them all is the power He placed down on the inside of me. I can therefore say without hesitation that I would not trade that change for a million dollars! And I mean that! Just read on.

Back toward the end of 1992 God began directing Lindsay and I to get more grounded in what was going on at Oral Roberts University. I had been the Executive Vice President there for some time. He also told us to go off daily television for a while. Now that was hard to swallow. We had been on for nearly nine years so you could imagine we were surprised to say the least. But just a few weeks after we went off, my father, Oral Roberts, had a heart attack. Then shortly after that, he stepped down as President and Corporate Executive Officer of the university.

That same week, the university board gathered to elect a new president. They voted unanimously to appoint me new president and

CEO of ORU. It was also during that week that my oldest daughter Cristi and her husband had their first baby, Kaitlin Victoria. Our first grandchild! In fact, Kaitlan was born right in the middle of my presidential inauguration ceremony.

But moments after Kaitlan was born, the doctors discovered she had swallowed too much fluid while in the birth canal. So they rushed her into intensive care. When I learned of this, I began to think back ten years earlier to the day when our little Richard Oral was born and died after only thirty-six hours: God quickly reminded Lindsay and I of His promise made back then. "You will not walk through that valley again." God said it, so we believed Him, and a peace came into our hearts. Not much later, Kaitlan was released from the hospital with a clean bill of health.

But this was just the beginning of many coming momentous events.

The day I was installed as CEO, I was officially given the financial responsibility of the university. I knew back in 1987 with all the things happening in ministries around the country and the negative coverage the media had given it, that most ministries had experienced drastic financial cuts. And ORU was no exception. But now I was looking at reports that showed we were $42 million dollars in debt! This was money we owed to creditors and companies who supplied the university with everyday things like light bulbs, paper towels, business supplies, and food for the students!

Somehow with fewer dollars coming in than before, we had to budget the daily needs of the the university and pay off this $42 million in debt. The monthly interest payment alone was tens of thousands!

I knew it would take some time to adjust to my university responsibilities while maintaining the TV ministry and my overseas travels. But nowhere in my wildest imagination did I expect the kind of pressure I now felt. It was literally like having a heavy ball chained to my neck, and every day I found it harder and harder to stay up.

Months went by and the pressure from creditors and bankers increased as I crept deeper and deeper into humiliation and despair.

At one point I did find that the university had stopped tithing to ministries and other works of the Lord as we had always done in the past. The administration just felt they could no longer afford to with all the debt hanging over their heads.

FAITH TO TRY AGAIN

I changed that immediately, and within a short amount of time miraculous things began to happen. We began to see a light at the end of the tunnel, but it was still a long way away. We had learned the meaning of believing and praying for our daily bread to see God move strongly on our behalf. But I was still feeling crushed under the weight of the responsibility.

In Second Corinthians Paul tells of a time when he felt this same heavy weight:

We were under great pressure, far beyond our ability to endure, so that we despaired even of life. Indeed, in our hearts we felt the sentence of death. But this happened that we might not rely on ourselves but on God, who raises the dead.

2 Corinthians 1:8-9 NIV

As was true for Paul, neither would God allow the weights and responsibilities of life to crush me.

I received an invitation to speak at Carpenter's Home Church from Pastor Karl Strader who is a member of the ORU Board of Regents. After receiving the invitation, Lindsay said the Lord had told her something new would start in my life because of this meeting. And she encouraged me to be expecting. Still, I had absolutely no idea of what God had waiting for me. What I found changed my life. It changed my family, the university, and anyone I come in contact with! The touch of God I received while at Karl Strader's church is so contagious that it cannot help but change anyone or anything that comes near me!

I do not have room here to tell all the details of this miraculous intervention of God, but I will say that God placed a supernatural joy within me! He gave me a joy that will not allow any circumstance to move me from believing God to move on my behalf. Nothing shakes me anymore. And as I have stood in faith trusting God and His Word to work on my behalf, I have seen miracle after miracle as the university has moved further and further out of debt. As of this writing we have seen God move over $21 million dollars from that seemingly insurmountable mountain of debt.

But more importantly, God has transformed me from a lifeless, hopeless shell of a man into a renewed, joy filled powerhouse for the kingdom of God. Now when faced with another creditor breathing down our neck, I no longer feel a stranglehold of defeat or depression. Instead, I open up my mouth and let out a belly shaking laugh with a deep sense of knowing that God is about to move again. Every time it appears in the natural that things are at an impasse,

God comes through at the last moment. Such pressure used to cause me so much stress that I literally got an ulcer. But now it makes me so happy I sometimes have to get up and dance because I know that I know that God is in control. He will not — He cannot fail!

Think About It.

Are you at a place in life where your circumstances seem so overwhelming at times that you find yourself wishing God would either take you home or hurry up and come back to get us all? Do you find that life has its up times, but even when they come you are hardly moved by them? Do you find it increasingly harder to laugh at anything?

Then maybe it's time you experienced the joy the Lord intended His children to walk in while here on the earth. Nehemiah 8:10 says,

"The joy of the Lord is your strength." That means, as Christians, our strength is the joy of the Lord. Without it we are powerless. How can Christians be content in the face of the attacks of Satan if we are not filled with God's power of joy? We can't!

My friend I wish with all my heart that every believer could experience the Holy Ghost joy and laughter that has flooded into my life. It has truly changed me. And I know it will change anyone who experiences it. The Bible says in Isaiah 40:31:

> *But they that wait upon the Lord shall renew their strength;*
> *they shall mount up with wings as eagles; they shall run, and not*
> *be weary; and they shall walk, and not faint.*

As you wait upon the Lord and linger in His presence, you will find yourself being filled with His wonderful joy. Psalm 16:11 says that in His presence is fullness of joy. When we wait upon the Lord and bask in His presence, we are like a jet plane getting refueled with high-octane fuel. We get refueled and ready to go anywhere to do anything He asks us to do.

Are you ready for the change of a lifetime? Are you ready to revolutionize the way you look at life and really make a difference in the kingdom of God? Then I encourage you—no I dare you—to seek the Lord and don't give up! Don't give in until He fills you with His joy unspeakable that is full of His glory!

FAITH TO SEEK GOD

And they that know thy name will put their trust in thee: for thou, LORD, hast not forsaken them that seek thee.
Psalm 9:10

Ask, and it shall be given you; seek and ye shall find; knock, and it shall be opened unto you...

Matthew 7:7

How can you overcome the kind of shocking news in your life that shatters all hope of deliverance? How can you break through that terrible crisis moment when your very insides feel like they're being torn apart and desolation sweeps over your soul? How can you rise above those times when you're plunged into misery and torment, and terror has you in its awful grip and you feel like you just can't break through to God?

There is a dramatic scene from the Bible in Isaiah 38, where King Hezekiah lay in his bedchamber violently ill. The prospect of death was hanging over him when the prophet Isaiah announced,

FAITH TO TRY AGAIN

Set thine house in order: for thou shalt die, and not live.

Isaiah 38:1

Isaiah was pronouncing a death sentence on the king by the Spirit of the Lord!

No doubt Hezekiah could feel the fear churning in the pit of his stomach as terror swept over him. He knew he was facing a choice. He could simply accept that death sentence as his final word and give up in despair. Or he could throw himself upon the mercy of the Lord and pray!

You say, "Oh, but the word of the Lord came to him through the prophet."

Yes, but there are times in our lives when God speaks to warn us about a certain thing so we can pray about it and avert a disaster!

FAITH TO TRY AGAIN

This was the kind of word King Hezekiah received from the Lord. And the only thing that could prevent that word from coming to pass was Hezekiah himself!

So what did Hezekiah do? The Bible says He turned his face to the wall and cried out to the Lord in prayer! He didn't waste a single moment in blotting out everything except God's goodness from his mind and heart. Then he began to plead his case before God! He cried,

Remember now, O Lord, I beseech thee, how I have walked before thee in truth and with a perfect heart, and have done that which is good in thy sight.

Isaiah 38:3

Now Hezekiah was in no way trying to justify himself before God. He was simply declaring that even if he had slipped and fallen at times, and made many mistakes, his heart was pure and honest before the Lord. The Bible says God does not judge us according to outward appearances! First Samuel 16:7 boldly proclaims, God looks on the heart!

The Bible says that Hezekiah began to weep. And it wasn't just a few tears that came rolling down his cheeks. The Bible says, he "wept sore." Hezekiah wasn't playing around with the desperation of his situation! He wasn't sending up some little weak-kneed, half-hearted prayer that barely reached to the ceiling! He was praying a gut-wrenching, soul-stirring, earthshaking, heaven-moving prayer to Almighty God! He was crying out to the Lord in his terrible anguish! He was praying an effectual, fervent prayer like the apostle James talks about in James 5:16!

Then, in the flash of a second, the prophet Isaiah burst through the doors of the king's bed chamber with a word hot off the wire from God.

FAITH TO TRY AGAIN

Thus saith the Lord, the God of David thy father, I have heard thy prayer, I have seen thy tears: behold, I will add unto thy days fifteen years.

Isaiah 38:5

God not only heard Hezekiah's heartfelt prayer, He also saw his tears. He saw that Hezekiah meant business. He saw the burning intensity of his prayer!

And that means you and I can't just breathe a little lukewarm, fainthearted prayer to God in the midst of your crisis and expect God's miracles to suddenly come raining down! We've got to stir ourselves up! We've got to shake off those feelings of apathy and weariness of heart! We've got to cut loose and pray a fervent, boiling-hot prayer! A prayer of such red-hot intensity that it shakes the devil's kingdom and the kingdom of God too! We've got to let both God and the devil himself know that we mean business!

King Hezekah's story is more than just a story from the Bible. It's the story of your life when you receive that terrible diagnosis or some other situation that makes it look like it's all over. It's the story of your life when the hurt and the cry inside you are ripping through your soul as you turn your face to God.

It's the story of your deliverance as you lift your eyes above the devil's alarming circumstances, to God your Deliverer to believe in Him alone!

It's time to shut the door on the doubters, scoffers and mockers!

We are living in a day when countless thousands of people are staggering under an overwhelming burden of debt. Second Kings 4 tells the dramatic story of a woman whose life was caught in the stranglehold of debt!

Now this woman was a widow. And in the midst of her grief, her husband's creditor had threatened to take her sons as slaves as payment for her debts. The Bible says she cried out to Elisha the prophet for help and that he gave her a divine plan of deliverance! Isn't that exactly what you're seeking from the Lord—His divine plan for your deliverance?

Well, Elisha told her to borrow as many vessels as she could from all her neighbors. Then he told her to take the little bit of oil she had left in her house and start pouring it into empty vessels. After she had done this, the Bible says she rushed back home and shut the door!

Why did she shut the door? First of all, she shut out the outside world. The world will never understand the supernatural act of your faith that unlocks the realm of God's blessing in your life! Second, she shut out the devil's crowd, because the devil's crowd will always mock and jeer at the divine intervention of Holy Ghost power!

So she shut out her friends and neighbors, because oftentimes even the ones who are the closest to us do not understand the miraculous plan of God for our lives.

This woman decided to do what King Hezekiah did. She turned her face to the wall, shut the door on the gainsayers and naysayers, and she got alone with God. And when she got alone with the One who scooped out the beds for the oceans, flung the stars from His fingertips, piled high the mountains, and dug deep the gorges, how her little house must have begun to rumble and shake!

I can see her now with the eyes of my spirit, dancing around the kitchen as the Lord filled every one of those empty vessels to overflowing with oil! And the Bible says when the widow sold the oil, she and her sons had enough money to pay their debts, with plenty left over to meet their daily needs!

Think About It.

Who are you looking to for victory today?

Let me ask you a penetrating question, my friend: Who or what besides God are you looking to for that life-changing, soul-shaking miracle of victory that you've just got to have today? Who or what are you clinging to besides the Savior? This widow's story and the story of King Hezekiah's deliverance encourage us to have enough grit—enough holy-dogged determination—enough of the Holy Ghost in us—to get hold of the Lord and refuse to turn loose! No matter our situation!

It's time for us to turn our face to the wall. It's time to shut the door on the doubters and the scoffers and the mockers! It's time to focus on Jesus and awaken to the fact that He's more than a match for the devil's roar! We've got to exchange our little halfhearted way of praying for God's bold-hearted way! And it's time to abandon ourselves to believe God all the way. God's Word is true!

Let me close with these encouraging words from the book of Romans. Read these words, over and over until they begin to sink in.

FAITH TO TRY AGAIN

Let God's Word and love give you, as He did for me, FAITH TO TRY AGAIN.

Therefore, there is now no condemnation for those who are in Christ Jesus, because through Christ Jesus the law of the Spirit of life set me free from the law of sin and death.

And we know that in all things God works for the good of those who love him, who have been called according to his purpose.

What, then, shall we say in response to this? If God is for us, who can be against us?

He who did not spare his own Son, but gave him up for us all--how will he not also, along with him, graciously give us all things?

FAITH TO TRY AGAIN

...in all these things we are more than conquerors through him who loved us.

Romans 8:1, 28, 31-32, 37 NIV

TRY AGAIN FAITH

Now faith is the substance of things hoped for, the evidence of things not seen. For by it the elders obtained a good report.

Through faith we understand that the worlds were framed by the word of God, so that things which are seen were not made of things which do appear.

By faith Abel offered unto God a more excellent sacrifice than Cain, by which he obtained witness that he was righteous, God testifying of his gifts: and by it he being dead yet speaketh.

By faith Enoch was translated that he should not see death; and was not found, because God had translated him: for before his translation he had this testimony, that he pleased God.

But without faith it is impossible to please him: for he that cometh to God must believe that he is, and that he is a rewarder of them that diligently seek him.

By faith Noah, being warned of God of things not seen as yet, moved with fear, prepared an ark to the saving of his house; by the which he condemned the world, and became heir of the righteousness which is by faith.

By faith Abraham, when he was called to go out into a place which he should after receive for an inheritance, obeyed; and he went out, not knowing whither he went....For he looked for a city which hath foundations, whose builder and maker is God.

Hebrews 11:1-8,10

About the Author

Since 1980, **Richard Roberts** has conducted evangelistic crusades on six continents. Whether he is conducting a healing crusade in a war-torn nation, or co-hosting with his wife, Lindsay, on their powerful daily television program, **Something Good TODAY with Richard and Lindsay** — the driving force behind his evangelistic outreach is the compassion of Jesus.

Richard holds a B.A. in Communication Arts and an M.A. in Theology from Oral Roberts University where he serves as president and CEO. He is also on the Board of Regents and is president of the Oral Roberts Evangelistic Association. Richard resides with his wife, Lindsay, in Tulsa, Oklahoma.

For information on other books
offered by Albury Publishing, write:

Albury Publishing
P.O. Box 470406
Tulsa, Oklahoma 74147-0406